Sheila Walsh

You're Worth It!

HARVEST HOUSE PUBLISHERS
EUGENE, OREGON

Cover by Harvest House Publishers Inc., Eugene, OR

Published in association with the literary agency of The FEDD Agency, Inc., PO Box 341973, Austin, TX 78734.

YOU'RE WORTH IT!

Copyright © 2015 Sheila Walsh
Published by Harvest House Publishers
Eugene, Oregon 97402
www.harvesthousepublishers.com

ISBN 978-0-7369-6385-5 (hardcover)
ISBN 978-0-7369-6386-2 (eBook)

Printed in China

15 16 17 18 19 20 21 22 23 / RDS-JH / 10 9 8 7 6 5 4 3 2 1

Contents

Are not two sparrows sold for a penny?
Yet not one of them will fall to the
ground outside your Father's care.
And even the very hairs of your
head are all numbered.
So don't be afraid; ***you are worth***
more than many sparrows.

MATTHEW 10:29-31

A Greeting from Sheila

I believe within the heart of every woman is a deep desire to be fully loved and accepted for who she is. To feel *worthy*. I believe we all desire the security and affirmation of a love and acceptance that cannot fail. If we're married, our husbands can only give us a limited measure of this kind of love. Loving parents, good friends, and beloved sisters in Christ can also do their part...but in the final analysis, it's just not enough. There is only one source for this kind of love and acceptance we crave— and that's in God, our creator and heavenly Father.

How do I know this desire for that kind of love is a nearly universal quest for women? I know it in part because I want that kind of love.

I also know it because for the past two decades I've ministered to more than five million women from every walk of life through our Women of Faith conferences. Six of us women formed a team in 1996 to travel to approximately 20 cities a year where we have listened, sung, worshipped, laughed, cried, and shared our hearts with other women. Some I visited in prison, some are June Cleaver moms, some are successful businesswomen. Some are brand-new Christians, others are seasoned veterans of the faith. All are different in many ways, but all have the same desire to feel valued...*worthy*.

Many of these women pray, attend Bible studies, they may teach Sunday School...and yet there's something vital missing from their faith. They will rarely speak to friends about it—they think they're the only ones who feel as they do. But they speak to me about it. They privately acknowledge that their present Christian experience simply isn't enough. There must be more...but what?

When you think about it, it's odd that we should feel this way. After all, we women work hard at what we do. If we have a job, we give our all to our bosses. If we're moms, we do our best to raise good kids. If we're wives, we try to meet our husband's needs as we hope he'll meet ours. If we have responsibilities at our church, we plunge right in to fulfill our calling.

Many of us have additional responsibilities unique to us. We may care for an aging parent or we may deal with adult children who have chosen the wrong path. Our grandchildren may need us in a way we had never anticipated. If we're single, it seems like we pull double duty, performing tasks that could be cut in half if only we had a spouse.

With all that goes on in our busy lives, is it any wonder that so many of us are tired, discouraged, and, despite all we do, still feeling unloved, unfulfilled, unworthy? And yet is that the way God wants us to see ourselves?

No, I'm certain it's not.

Like many of you, I've walked the walk. Shame, *yes*. Confusion, *check*. Questions, *yep*. Depression, *oh yes*! Frustration, *amen to that too*.

But because I've walked the walk, I've also been able to discover some answers—God's answers—to my feelings of unworthiness and unloveliness. In this short book, I'd like you to take a journey with me. This journey begins where we are right now, right this very minute, and will take us past feelings of worry, doubt, rejection, shame, confusion, and all the other negative (and wrong!) self-perceptions we have.

> Because I've walked the walk, I've also been able to discover some answers—God's answers—to my feelings of unworthiness and unloveliness.

If deep in your heart there is a fervent desire to be known and accepted and loved and valued for who you are just as you are, please come with me on our brief journey. Despite all you may feel now, *you are worthy!*

1

Our Secret Self

*Somewhere in the side streets of our soul
is a place where [our] secret self lives.*

MIKE YACONELLI

Within us is the secret place where the doubting, condemning, and self-nagging come from. Where defeating voices accuse us of being worthless to God. They're constantly telling us we don't measure up to some phantom image we have of a Super Christian Woman who never fails, always looks as if she stepped out of a magazine, and whose house makes Martha Stewart look like a slacker.

Please be advised the phantom Super Christian Woman does not exist. You are not her. I'm *certainly* not her.

> Please be advised
> the phantom Super
> Christian Woman does
> not exist. You are not her.
> I'm *certainly* not her.

Although I don't know the exact words your secret self uses to undermine your worth, I know mine. I know how they came to be too. Some of you already know my story, but for those who don't, perhaps this is the place to tell you how early tragic events in my life caused me to build a secret self that would one day cause my world to crumble.

When I was five years old, my father was in a car accident that may have contributed to a blood clot that eventually caused a massive brain aneurism and precipitated a marked personality change. Dad became violent and had to be taken to a psychiatric hospital where he died at his own hand. My dad's death took its toll on our entire family—including me. Because of my dad's brain injury and the unreasonable anger he directed toward me, I was convinced he hated me. To feel the brunt of your own father's anger (and lack of love) is very destructive to a child. It was to me. It affected me profoundly, following me into my adult years.

At age eleven, I committed myself to Christ, yet my pain of having an earthly father who seemingly hated me caused me to remain fearful. I wondered, would my heavenly Father ever turn on me as my own earthly father had?

The Sanctuary of God's Word

At that young age, I began to take refuge in the powerful verses of Psalm 91. Many of you know this psalm as well as I do. You, too, have made it your pillow when you've been overwhelmed.

> He who dwells in the secret place of the Most High
> Shall abide under the shadow of the Almighty.
> I will say of the LORD, "He is my refuge and my fortress;
> My God, in Him I will trust."
>
> Surely He shall deliver you from the snare of the fowler
> And from the perilous pestilence.
> He shall cover you with His feathers,
> And under His wings you shall take refuge;
> His truth shall be your shield and buckler.
> You shall not be afraid of the terror by night,
> Nor of the arrow that flies by day,
> Nor of the pestilence that walks in darkness,
> Nor of the destruction that lays waste at noonday.

A thousand may fall at your side,
And ten thousand at your right hand;
But it shall not come near you.
Only with your eyes shall you look,
And see the reward of the wicked.

Because you have made the LORD, who is my refuge,
Even the Most High, your dwelling place,
No evil shall befall you,
Nor shall any plague come near your dwelling;
For He shall give His angels charge over you,
To keep you in all your ways.
In their hands they shall bear you up,
Lest you dash your foot against a stone.
You shall tread upon the lion and the cobra,
The young lion and the serpent you shall
trample underfoot.

"Because he has set his love upon Me,
therefore I will deliver him;
I will set him on high, because he has known My name.
He shall call upon Me, and I will answer him;
I will be with him in trouble;
I will deliver him and honor him.
With long life I will satisfy him,
And show him My salvation."

New King James Version

We can't read this psalm without pausing from verse to verse and taking in the love and protection it offers. The God of Psalm 91 is our high tower, our refuge, our strength. I'm grateful that my young heart believed in God's fierce love because later, as an adult, I would desperately need to cling to that love.

> The God of Psalm 91
> is our high tower,
> our refuge, our strength.

The Unveiling of the Secret Self

Fast-forward through several years of successful music ministry, including several bestselling albums and TV appearances. By age 36 in 1992, I had reached the heights. I was a "Christian celebrity," hosting a popular TV show on CBN. Little did I know my secret self was about to come crashing down. Up till then, I honestly (and quite wrongly) thought my successful ministry would somehow negate the feelings of shame, fear, and unworthiness I had endured for so long.

It all came tumbling down when I was hospitalized at North Virginia Doctor's Hospital for a month and diagnosed with severe dysthymic disorder. In short: clinical depression. My father had died in a psychiatric hospital while in his thirties. And now was the same thing happening to me in *my* thirties? Was I on a collision course with an early death? Needless to say, I was terrified.

Much to my dismay, the doctor prescribed medication. Not just for my hospital stay, but ongoing medication. Ongoing as in I still take it more than twenty years later. I always will.

Does that make me less of a Christian? Are you now disappointed to hear that I wasn't dramatically healed and will never need medication again? I hope not...but I have to tell you that some of my friends were disappointed in me. To admit to my weakness was somehow not consistent with a "woman of faith." How ironic! I've now been a speaker for Women of Faith almost as long as I've been taking medication.

Are some of you closing the book now? Please don't.

The Gift of Our Wounds

At one point after being on medication for more than a decade, I decided to quit taking it. Would anyone notice? Would *I* notice? Leave it to God to have my husband, Barry, notice. After a couple of weeks, it was apparent to Barry that I had not been taking my medication. I was more withdrawn, quiet, sad. I was so disappointed. Why hadn't God healed me? Must my medication become a daily reminder of my brokenness for the rest of my life?

God said yes. It wasn't overnight, but eventually I came to the place where I prayed this prayer:

Father,

Who am I to tell you how you should heal me? I know you could touch me in a moment and I would be completely restored, but if you never do that I will daily thank you for the provision and help available in this broken world. If I am left with this internal limp so that I can recognize it in another, then I thank you for that. You are good and you are God, all the time. All the time! Amen.

> If I am left with this internal limp so that I can recognize it in another, then I thank you for that.

I came to terms with the knowledge that in this area of my life, my brokenness would be on display to all who knew me well for the rest of my life. No one I know plans for such a life event. No one wants to feel like there's a tender area of their life which might cause someone to question your faith. If you know someone who fights depression, don't use that as a measure of their faith. And if that person is you, don't you let it affect your worth before God. If the truth were known, I suspect every woman—and every man—on the planet has some internal limp they never planned on.

Prayer Invitation

Before you move on to chapter two, I want you to do something. I want you to stop and think about your secret self. Then I want you to pray out loud and as you pray, I want you to name specific aspects of your secret self you know are holding you back. You might choose words like *failure, fear, lack of confidence, anger, memories*, or a thousand other words.

Go!

2

God Knows Our Whole Story

*The Christian does not think God will love
us because we are good, but that God will
make us good because He loves us.*

C.S. LEWIS

I met a woman recently—I literally bumped into her—at the airport and she said something that brought a knowing smile to my face. She was carrying so many bags and was in such a hurry that we collided as I exited the coffee shop. After we apologized to each other, I stopped to help her pick up her stuff.

"If you think this is a lot," she said, "you should see what I'm carrying on the inside!"

She laughed as she headed off to her gate, but there was something in the tone of her voice that resonated with me. Don't we all carry something on the inside that others may never see? Something that weighs us down. Burdens us.

Could it be that something (or some*things*) in your life's journey have left you with those burdens? If so, let me say to you what God has said to me: "I love you, my daughter, more than you'll ever realize. Your burden, your internal limp is nothing but a reminder that your strength and purpose and worth come from me, not from your own sufficiency."

It took a crisis of grace to set me straight. And it wasn't painless, believe me. Pain seems to be an inevitable part of making us willing to ditch our secret selves and find true freedom in Christ. No more striving, no more pretending, no more wondering if God is satisfied with our efforts to please him. Grace from God to free us from both our secret self and grace to put to death the phantom Super Christian Woman. Neither of those women is the true you.

News flash: God knows all about our secret self, and he loves—*cherishes*—us anyway. He was there during the tragic time of my father's mental breakdown and eventual suicide. He saw what it did to me. He saw and he waited. But never once during that awful time was God absent. Never once was his love toward me less than sufficient. Never once did those events affect my standing with God.

The problem was I didn't know that then.

Now I can look back and see the trail of bread crumbs that led to my crisis, starting with my father's tragic death.

> God knows all about our secret self, and he loves—*cherishes*—us anyway.

Fully Known, Fully Loved

I'm intrigued by some of the women in the Bible Jesus ministered to. We don't often get to see their trail of bread crumbs either—we just know that they, like us, have a past that Jesus knows all about and he intervenes in their life anyway.

In John 4 we meet a woman whose name we never know. We simply refer to her as the Samaritan woman. What we do know, we tend to frown on. After all, she had been married five times and, when Jesus met her, she was living with a man who was not her husband. It's hard not to think of her as the Elizabeth Taylor of her day. The truth is, all we are given is a glimpse into one afternoon in her life, and we don't know how she got there. We are not privy to her trail of bread crumbs.

I do think there are some things we can surmise, though. For instance, it wasn't likely her Plan A in life to have five-going-on-six husbands. I don't know of any young woman who starts off hoping to marry five times.

I imagine she married for the first time when she was thirteen or fourteen, as was the custom. I like to think it was a love match, perhaps a boy whose eye she caught one day across the busy market streets. It would appear that she had no children, and in those days that was perceived as a curse from God. Perhaps that was why her first marriage ended. Her husband would simply tell her, "You are free." What that really meant was, "You are homeless." He had no obligation to provide for her in any way.

In time she met another man and once more she hoped that this time love would be strong enough to withstand any storm...but it was not to be. By the time we meet her, she has five marriages under her belt and is now simply grateful to have a roof over her head. I imagine her to be one of the loneliest women alive, weighed down by an overcoat of shame.

John tells us that she fetched water at the sixth hour, which is noon by a Palestinian clock. None of the other women of her village would have been there at that hour, when the sun was at its hottest. There's nothing worse than being a woman with a reputation in a small town.

In his study of John's Gospel, William Barclay tells us that this well is half a mile outside of the woman's village of Sychar. Sychar had water of its own, but she chose to make this daily, lonely trek away from the disapproving glances of others. She had no way of knowing as she set off on that day that all her secrets were about to be exposed by the One who knows everything there is to know.

She was shocked when Jesus spoke to her. No self-respecting rabbi or teacher would address a woman in public. Not only that, she was a Samaritan, a group despised by Jews...but then, Jesus came for those despised by others. When he asked her to go and fetch her husband, I wonder if she wanted to laugh or cry? She simply said, "I have no husband."

Jesus could have left it there. Why add to her shame? But he said, "You are right when you say you have no husband. The fact is, you have had five husbands, and the man you now have is not your husband. What you have just said is quite true."

Well there it is! All her dirty laundry suspended in the noonday heat.

Why do you think Jesus did that?

Did he want to shame her?

Was he mad at her?

No, that's not who he is.

God is not mad at you either.

I believe that this is one of the most important truths for us to grasp hold of.

Unless we believe that Jesus knows every dirty little secret we keep and loves us anyway, we will never understand the depth of this great love. God is aware of every step and misstep we've taken to reach his presence and is *still* overjoyed to see us. We are cherished.

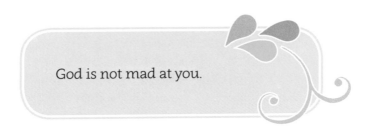

God is not mad at you.

Where Grace Leads

The radical, grace-filled message of the gospel is that God knows every single thing about us and in spite of it all, still passionately and intentionally loves us. We get to bring our secret self to the cross and to the party God throws for all his children. This is where grace comes in. Grace from God to free us from our secret self and grace to put to death the phantom Super Christian Woman. Neither of those women is the true you.

Now, what about your trail of bread crumbs? What has so affected you that you have assumed a secret self that is not really yourself at all? Are you ready to finally give up that shadow that isn't you? Aren't you ready to live with the reality that in God's eyes you are worth the death of his beloved son?

That's really what it's all about. Realizing that God painfully (yes, I believe it pained God for his son to hang on that cross of torture) surrendered the life of Jesus for *you*.

As for your secret self, God knows all about it. We can no more hide from God behind a secret self than Adam and Eve could hide from him in the garden.

Whatever you're going through now, whatever is robbing you of your sense of worth in your own eyes, can I reassure you that in God's eyes, you are worthy of the death of his Son? What greater evidence could God offer to demonstrate your worth? Then, knowing the value God has placed on you, can you really dare to ascribe less worth to yourself than he does?

My story is not your story. So, no, this is not about dealing with depression. Depression was the path that brought me to the end of myself and to the beginning of a fresh experience with God. An experience through which I saw (and am still seeing) my worth to God. Your story will be different. But the one thing I will assume we have in common with each other and with millions of other Christian women is that we battle with believing we are worthy of the love and acceptance God offers us.

Prayer Invitation

Stand with Jesus, not as Super Christian Woman, but as the real you. Think about the steps and missteps you've taken that have brought you to his feet. Can you hold those with thankfulness for that reason? As you pray today, offer words of praise for your *whole* story.

3

The Fear of Rejection

Blessed are the poor in spirit, for theirs is the kingdom of heaven. Blessed are those who mourn, for they will be comforted. Blessed are the meek, for they will inherit the earth.

MATTHEW 5:3-5

Have you ever thought, *If people really knew me, they would reject me?* Maybe those weren't the exact words, but at some point you've been very glad that others can't see inside you—read your thoughts, take a stroll down your memory lane, or get a glimpse of where your mind wanders when you can't sleep at night.

Rejection is a powerful weapon in the hands of our enemy. You do have an enemy, you know. He's the "accuser of the brethren," constantly nagging us with thoughts like...

You'll never amount to anything.

You'll never measure up to other women.

Why would anyone choose to love you?

You should be ashamed of your secret thoughts!

Though I believe the enemy of our souls has many weapons designed to rob us of our worth, surely one of the most potent is inflicting a sense of rejection on us. If he can find an opportunity to do so, he will help each of us build a secret self through instances of real or perceived rejection. But God shows us in his Word and through his tender work in our lives that when we trust him, no matter what is happening around us, we will receive, again and again, reminders of his great love and our great worth in his eyes.

> We will receive, again and again, reminders of his great love and our great worth in his eyes.

Changed by His Light

I can think of no other person who so profoundly understood the depths of fear and rejection and the power of Christ's love than Mary Magdalene.

She had been possessed by seven demons. We don't know how long she had lived like this before her encounter with Christ, but can you imagine even for a moment what that must have been like? Not only did she live in fear, but she was likely feared and rejected by everyone.

In his great mercy, God's love propels him to what might seem to us like ridiculous lengths to rescue one tormented person, even when they don't have the presence of mind to ask for help. Mary understood the reaches of God's love. From the moment of her deliverance, her devotion to Christ was unwavering.

Mary had tasted the worst that any broken soul can experience and she knew that with one word from Christ all the evil that had plagued her for years had to leave. As followers of Christ we cannot be possessed, but there are fears that can become our demons.

When we feel ruled by those demons, we do have choices. We can embrace faith in the power of Christ as Mary did. And we can move forward in our healing with pure devotion.

Love for the Least of These

Think for a minute about how often Jesus sought out the rejected ones. The woman at the well, Matthew and Zacchaeus (both tax collectors), blind Bartimaeus, lepers, the demon-possessed, the use of a dreaded Samaritan as the hero in one of his parables...even Saul, a staunch Pharisee whom most of us would quickly reject.

There's no getting around it: God loves what the world rejects. His hobby is redeeming rejection. That's the good news. But there's also a danger associated with rejection. There's always the chance for us to become comfortable in our rejection. It becomes our norm. We're no longer surprised when others don't choose us or when we're targeted for criticism. In some odd way, we've come to expect rejection as our lot. We think we deserve to be rejected.

That's a sad mindset we must pull away from. Let me offer an example from my own life that really surprised me when it was pointed out.

For the longest time, when someone would compliment me on my singing, my message, my ministry, or even the way I was dressed, I would quickly deflect the compliment with an offhand remark that undercut their praise. It was very hard for my secret self to accept words of praise. Oddly, if someone had been critical of something I did or the way I looked, I would have somehow felt deserving of the barb. When you become accustomed to your perceived lack of worth, compliments are unbelieved and unreceived while criticism is accepted as your due.

I suppose my willingness to accept rejection went back to those dark days of my childhood as I recalled the way my own father rejected me. Parental rejection can be the hardest rejection to overcome. As children, we're so innocent, so believing. When someone in authority says something, we're inclined to believe them. A child who is told she's stupid or ugly or awkward will very likely carry those words with her for a very long time. They will help form her sense of identity—for better or for worse.

The Beauty of Broken Vessels

When I was a student in London, one of my favorite places to shop was the Reject China Shop. It was next to Harrods, that grand luxury department store. The Reject China Shop sold the cups and dishes and mugs that didn't pass Harrods's eagle-eyed inspection. As a student on a budget I admired the china Harrods sold but went shopping next door to save money.

One day I decided to see if I could find a perfect mug that had slipped through by mistake. I was on a quest. I held mug after mug up to the light, but each time I would see a chip or a flaw, a tiny crack beneath the glaze. But then I found a beautiful, flawless piece. I bought it and took it back to my apartment, anxiously awaiting my first cup of perfect tea.

The minute the water was on the requisite British rolling boil, I poured it into the mug and watched in disbelief as a crack suddenly appeared from top to bottom. It had been imperceptible until the heat exposed it.

I'll never forget that moment. As I looked at the unusable piece of china I thought, "This is a picture of your life, Sheila. Oh sure you look good on the outside but one day, when it gets too hot, you're going to fall apart just like this mug." That was my identity: a cracked young woman who deserved any rejection she got. I was the star attraction at the Reject Sheila Walsh Shop.

When we experience rejection as a child, it's hard not to see it around every corner. My dad's brain injury and subsequent violence left me scarred as a five-year-old child. I was no longer fit for Harrods; I'd have to live next door.

I wonder what messages you've carried inside you for so long that they seem true?

Were you told you weren't wanted?

Or that you should have been a boy?

Has someone made it clear that you're not as smart or as pretty as your sister?

Whatever the message, the scar runs deep, but praise God, the gospel runs deeper!

Paul addressed these killer beliefs of rejection in his letter to the Church in Rome: "What, then, shall we say in response to these things? If God is for us, who can be against us?" (Romans 8:31).

No matter how many times we're rejected in this broken world, the everlasting arms of our Father are always open, always loving, always here.

> The scar runs deep,
> but praise God, the
> gospel runs deeper!

While rejection can be real and overt, it may only be perceived. Even then it can be as harmful as open rejection. A child whose parent dies or goes off to war may misinterpret the absence as rejection, even when the child is dearly loved and accepted by the missing parent. That can hurt as much as being the last child chosen for the team.

Maybe your childhood was full of acceptance, but you faced rejection as an adult. Perhaps your husband left you for someone else. Maybe an adult child whom you love dearly has rejected you and gone off on his or her own, leaving you, like the father of the prodigal son, watching for his return. Maybe you were rejected professionally—passed over for advancement by someone younger or prettier or more aggressive.

In the worst-case scenario, maybe you feel like it's God himself who has rejected you. How odd when we consider how very harshly Jesus himself felt rejection from his people (see John 1:11). Yes, God understands rejection.

And God chooses broken vessels to fill with his ever-flowing love and healing.

Diving into God's Deep Love

What do we do with our rejection? How can we find worth amidst a sea of rejection?

Two things will help us. First, we search out the truth of God's Word regarding his acceptance of us. Second, we sink into those truths with the full weight of our body and soul, our past and our future, and our burdens. Here are a few diving boards to get you started:

> Though my father and mother forsake me,
> the LORD will receive me (Psalm 27:10).

> For you created my inmost being;
> you knit me together in my mother's womb.
> I praise you because I am fearfully and wonderfully made;
> your works are wonderful,
> I know that full well.
> My frame was not hidden from you
> when I was made in the secret place,
> when I was woven together in the depths of the earth
> (Psalm 139:13-15).

> Come to me, all you who are weary and burdened, and I will give you rest. Take my yoke upon you and learn from me, for I am gentle and humble in heart, and you will find rest for your souls. For my yoke is easy and my burden is light (Matthew 11:28-30).

> Blessed be the God and Father of our Lord Jesus Christ, who has blessed us with every spiritual blessing in the heavenly places in Christ, just as He chose us in Him before the foundation of the world, that we should be holy and without blame before Him in love, having predestined us to adoption as sons by Jesus Christ to Himself, according

to the good pleasure of His will, to the praise of the glory of His grace, *by which He made us accepted in the Beloved* (Ephesians 1:3-6 NKJV).

God demonstrates his own love for us in this: While we were still sinners, Christ died for us (Romans 5:8).

We love because he first loved us (1 John 4:19).

After we sink into the great depths of God's loving words, we can immerse ourselves in the healing love of God. Not as a point of theology, but as our own reality. The reality of God's personal and private love for us individually. For *you* individually. In other words, we must make the good news of Christ's love for us extremely personal. It wasn't just for "the world" that Christ died. It was for *me*. God has placed a value on my life and that value is the life of Christ. In short, we are each worth to God the most valuable possession of all: his Son.

If that doesn't bring forth a "Wow!" nothing will!

> We must make the good news of Christ's love for us extremely personal.

Prayer Invitation

As you end this chapter, I want you to acknowledge any known roots of rejection in your life, either real or perceived. Name them out loud as you reject rejection. Then turn at least two of the verses I've listed above into short prayers of acceptance.

4

Receiving God's Love

Turn around and believe that the good news that we are loved is better than we ever dared hope, and that to believe in that good news, to live out of it and toward it, to be in love with that good news, is of all glad things in this world the gladdest thing of all. Amen, and come Lord Jesus.

FREDERICK BUECHNER

It's hard to fully receive God's love when we're still battling rejection. But when rejection ceases to be an issue, we find that we have more capacity to receive God's love. And what a staggeringly beautiful day it is when that finally occurs.

I'll never forget an older woman I met at a Women of Faith conference. With tears pouring down her cheeks she told me she had been attending church, Bible studies, and home groups all her life. She had done her best to live a good life. But it was that night at that conference that she says she finally "got it." She told me, "Tonight I finally understand for the first time that God really loves me. It's just that simple. He loves me!"

While I was so happy to see her finally grasp the enormity of God's love for her, I couldn't help but wonder what her life could have been like if she had fully realized this love much earlier. I'm sure it would have affected her life—and her family—deeply. As I thought about and prayed for this woman over the next several days, I realized that she spoke for multitudes of women who dutifully sit in church every Sunday and go through the motions of the contemporary successful Christian woman, while on the inside she knows something is missing. But *what*?

This older woman finally discovered the "but what" when God's love was made real to her.

The power of God's love for each of us, when the light bulb goes on and we finally *see* the depths of that love, is life-changing. We go from seeing ourselves as just another woman on the planet to seeing ourselves as God's specially chosen daughter whom he loves more than any earthly father has ever loved a daughter.

> The power of God's love for each of us, when the light bulb goes on and we finally *see* the depths of that love, is life-changing.

The Source of Pure Love

I'm in awe of women who have known the affirming love of a good earthly father. That's something I've never experienced, nor will I ever have the chance to experience it. But as I continue to move past the rejection of my dad who at that point of his life was truly incapable of loving me as a normal father loves his daughter, I more fully bask in the love of my heavenly Father.

We know that the love of an earthly father is really just a picture of our heavenly Father's love. In a normal father/daughter relationship, a daughter should be able to see in her dad a glimpse of the greater love God has for her. So when the earthly example of a father's love is absent, it can be hard to grasp God's father-love for us.

Perhaps, though, the absence of that earthly paternal love propels women to seek it elsewhere. I could tell you stories that would curl your hair of women who sought to find the love of their father in the arms of men who used and abused them. Sadly, they were moved even farther from the source of true love and acceptance.

Perhaps the woman at the well I mentioned in chapter one was like that. What was she desperately seeking in the arms of six different men? Jesus, referring to the well, told her, "Whoever drinks of this water will thirst again, but whoever drinks of the water that I shall give him will never thirst. But the water that I shall give him will become in him a fountain of water springing up into everlasting life" (John 4:13-14 NKJV).

Thirsting for the Father's love is a good thing. I've had to come to the place of accepting the fact that, as tragic as it was to be unloved, even rejected by my father, it ultimately created in me a hunger for a father's love that was real and unchangeable. An unrelenting love. That, of course, led me to the discovery of God's love for me—after I was willing to abandon my secret self.

> Thirsting for the Father's love is a good thing.

As I was able to do that, here is possibly the most important thing I learned about God's love for me: His love is not dependent on me. Nor is it subject to change. There's nothing I can do to make God love me more and there's nothing I can do to make him love me less. His love is a perfect love, an endless love, a changeless love.

It's All God

The kind of endless, unstoppable, glorious, healing love Paul speaks of in Romans is the very kind of love we must, by God's grace, learn to receive.

> I am persuaded that neither death nor life, nor angels nor principalities nor powers, nor things present nor things to come, nor height nor depth, nor any other created thing, shall be able to separate us from the love of God which is in Christ Jesus our Lord (Romans 8:38-39 NKJV).

Believing in this pure, unconditional love is so hard for many of us. We are so oriented to earning love by how we behave. How we succeed. How we are perceived.

For me, as a performer on stage, I relate to being accepted by how well I have performed. I well remember during one of my very first concerts in America I gave a less-than-stellar performance. In fact, my manager told me as I exited the stage, "Well, that was disappointing!"

Indeed it was. I had failed. My performance was "off." It's been part of my experience—and possibly yours too—that our "performance" has a lot to do with how we perceive God's love toward us. If we, in fact, fail in some area of our life, we may wrongly believe God's opinion and commitment to us has changed. But God's love is dependent totally on him and who he is and has nothing to do with our performance. God's love isn't given because of what we've done or not done. In fact, God's love is given in spite of what we've done, where we've been, or who we are in our innermost thoughts. God has seen the movie of our life and he is not embarrassed by it. Every sin, every shameful thought, every failure, he has promised to forgive. Why? Because of the depth of his love for us. Redeeming love!

Not just our sins, but every single event that happens in our life, can, when entrusted to God, be redeemed by God's love. They can, in fact, reveal God's love.

> God's love is dependent totally on him and who he is and has nothing to do with our performance.

Darkness Gives Way to Light

One of my heroines is Joni Earekson Tada. For more than forty years, Joni has lived as a quadriplegic due to a diving accident when she was a teenager. Her life is limited by where she can go in her wheelchair. But in other ways, Joni's life is unlimited. She is far more productive, full, and adventurous than most women who have full range of motion. Not only is she a wonderful artist (and a fine singer too!), but she has allowed God to use the tragedy she suffered to draw her close to Christ and bring others close to him as well. Though I ache for the things Joni must miss due to her disability, I shudder when I think how many lives would be untouched today if she had not shared God's light in her darkness with the many thousands who have benefited from her ministry.

Where others see tragedy plunging a life into darkness, she found light. She has told me, in fact, that it was her wheelchair that taught her how to love Christ. Imagine that! God's love revealed through tragedy! That's redemption.

Sisters in Christ, make no mistake about it: God's love for us defies reason. It truly is an utterly unreasonable love.

> When the light of God's love becomes real to us, the darkness is dispelled.

A second lesson I've learned about God's love—and if you've been with me this far, it will come as no surprise: Sometimes God must allow us to go to a dark place so that we might finally come to his light. There are fewer darker places than a psychiatric hospital. And yet it was there that I came to my own end and the beginning of realizing that God, in loving me, could do for me what I could never do for myself.

I discovered the important connection between being grounded in God's love for me and accepting myself as a woman of worth.

Lean in! This is important: *When we're in dark places, we must remember that dark places must eventually give way to the light.* Darkness is, after all, the absence of light. When the light of God's love becomes real to us, the darkness is dispelled.

> God's love for us defies reason. It truly is an utterly unreasonable love.

Darkness is the enemy's territory. And he is forever seeking to counteract our apprehension of God's love. He loves to keep us in the dark room of self-pity, low self-esteem, and lack of confidence in ourselves, even though we are women for whom God gave his beloved son.

Just as darkness is dispelled by light, so too are lies dispelled by the truth. One of the hardest things I've had to do is embrace what is true about me and discard what is untrue.

Saved by Truth

I've already shared briefly my disappointment when I was released from the psychiatric hospital and my Christian "friends" began to express their sorrow over my "loss of faith." Clearly, in their minds, a woman of faith could not and would not suffer from depression. I fielded one such phone call that left me sitting on the floor in a puddle of tears. A friend had just inserted a new tape for me to replay in my mind—if I chose to—reminding me that good Christians are immune from depression. And weakness. And discouragement. And disappointment. And feelings of low self-worth.

I didn't stay on the floor in that puddle of tears long. Seeing my reflection in a mirror and not liking what I saw—a cowering, scared little girl—I stood up and began countering the lies of the enemy with words of truth. No longer would I allow the opinions of others to shape who I was. No longer would I cringe at the accusations of someone who had never walked in my shoes. No longer would I listen to the old recordings in my mind that told me I was worthless as a Christian, that God would never use me again, that I'd never find happiness.

In place of those worn-out lies, I began to believe about myself what God believes about me. I began to read the Bible out loud. (It's good for us to *hear* the Word of God.) I also began to write out verses that would become the new messages to set me free from the lies of the enemy. I posted these Scriptures where I would see them—on the refrigerator, on the dashboard, on the bathroom mirror. Verses from the Psalms were especially life-changing.

See, by now I was *determined* to fully apprehend God's love for me. It was a matter of my survival. And the way for me to apprehend God's love was to change the way I thought about myself and about God.

Belief Changes Everything

One of my favorite writers, A. W. Tozer, said, "What comes to your mind when you think about God is the most important thing about us."

That's quite a statement! If you think God is someone who disapproves of you, that thought will affect your ability to receive his love.

If you believe God keeps score of all your wrongs, then you're not free to enjoy his love.

If you think he has favorites, it will affect how you pray. If a prayer seems unanswered it will confirm your worst fears; God loves some of his children more than others.

If you think God is impressed when you present your better self, you'll never be able to bring your whole self to him.

If, however, you believe that almighty God, the one who spoke this world into being, who created all things beautiful, loves you with a fiery passion on your good days and your not-so-good days, then you will find yourself soaked to the skin in love and grace.

We are forever loved by God. Completely loved by God, passionately loved by God. When we understand this, we can finally trust him in a way we never have before. God's love fully realized in a woman's heart revolutionizes her life. Gone are the performance promises, the deflating comparisons with other women, the attempts to be something we were never meant to be—and, perhaps best of all, gone are the secret shames we've harbored for so long.

> God's love fully realized in a woman's heart revolutionizes her life.

Here's the thought I want to leave you with as this chapter closes: A love as outrageous as God's love for us begs for a response. How can we *not* respond to such a fierce, tenacious, relentless love?

When the great Scottish preacher and author George MacDonald (and one of my countrymen) was trying to explain the grace of God and the glories of eternity to his son, the boy replied that such a thing sounded too good to be true. The boy's wise father replied, "Nay, laddie. It's just so good, it *must* be true."

Indeed it must.

Prayer Invitation

This time I want you to pray out loud this prayer of acceptance of God's love for you.

Heavenly Father, I confess my lack of confidence in your love for me. I have both consciously and unconsciously erected barriers to anything more than just a head knowledge of your deep love. But now, by faith, I fully accept your love for me. I believe the blood of Christ has cleansed me from every sin. I believe that as your daughter, I'm free from the guilt, rejections, bitterness, and blame of the past. Help me to grow deeper and deeper in your love. May I never be forgetful or doubtful again that you value me as highly as the life of your son. Amen.

5

Forgiven and Forgiving

*To love means loving the unlovable. To
forgive means pardoning the unpardonable.
Faith means believing the unbelievable.*

G.K. CHESTERTON

One day when my son Christian was little, he asked me how much was seventy times seven. I replied that it was four hundred and ninety and asked him why he wanted to know.

"My teacher says that we have to forgive that many times," he replied.

"She's right," I said.

"But after 490 times, I don't have to forgive any more, right?" (I should have seen that one coming.)

I explained that we must forgive others as God forgives us—and that we need forgiveness far more than 490 times. That wasn't the answer he was looking for, as he told me he was quite sure he couldn't forgive one of his classmates that many times.

I know there are people in our lives like Christian's classmate. They've hurt us in the past or in the present and we don't like it. We don't want to forgive them. I know that feeling. But I also know that I have been forgiven by God far more often than I have had to forgive others. If 490 had been God's limit with me, I would have surpassed that number decades ago.

Forgive by Faith

When we struggle with unforgiveness, we need to look in the mirror and thank God we're beholding a fully forgiven person. Then we go and do likewise. Fully forgive. We do this by faith, not by feeling. By faith, we release our offender from their offense. Our feelings about the matter must be set aside. Faith never relies on feelings.

Although we forgive others because God instructs us to do so, we also reap a huge benefit in the act of forgiving: We buy our own freedom from the ongoing pain of harboring bitterness against the one who has offended us.

When Jesus was eating at a Pharisee's house, a woman "who had lived a sinful life" entered the room with an alabaster jar of expensive perfume. Luke reports that she "began to wet his feet with her tears. Then she wiped them with her hair, kissed them, and poured perfume on them" (Luke 7:38). The Pharisee host watched with disgust, thinking, *If this man were a prophet, he would know who is touching him and what kind of woman she is—that she is a sinner* (verse 39).

Jesus, of course, perceived what the Pharisee was thinking and replied with a parable. He concluded with "her many sins are forgiven—for she loved much. But he who has been forgiven little loves little." As the scene ends, Jesus tells the woman, "Your sins are forgiven…Your faith has saved you; go in peace."

To be forgiven is to be free. It's to go in peace.

To not receive forgiveness from God—or from others—is to remain in prison. We cannot enjoy God's love while we remain in the prison of unforgiveness.

We've explored how rejection is one of Satan's several strategies designed to destroy our sense of worth. Another of his most powerful weapons is convincing us to hold on to our offenses.

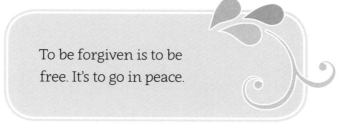

To be forgiven is to be free. It's to go in peace.

I've mentioned earlier that when I was in the psychiatric hospital, I had my version of Job's comforters. I specifically remember three of them, each of whom had their explanation for my condition. None of which comforted me in the least.

Later, after I was released, I realized I needed to forgive these people. Oh, I certainly didn't want to do this. It was agony. But I was determined to obey what I knew God wanted me to do. So I contacted all three, but was able to come to a place of understanding with only one of them. I'm sorry it turned out that way, but my obedience turned into a huge blessing for me. I *learned* how to forgive by faith, and forgiveness became the exit door from my interior prison of unworthiness.

There was someone else I had to forgive. At my doctor's suggestion I wrote a letter to my long-dead father. In this letter I expressed my anger and confusion at the change in him. But by the time I was finished, I was—to my surprise—overwhelmed not only by a desire to forgive him for the hurt, the rejection, the disappointment, but at rest remembering the dad who had loved me. There was healing for me in writing that letter.

God Can Handle Your Burdens

I've met many women who wrestle with unforgiveness. Whether their pain was caused by an unfaithful spouse, an abusive parent, an unfair advantage given to someone else, or something else, these women found forgiveness too difficult. But what that tells me is they haven't experienced full forgiveness from God for their own sins. When we understand our offense toward God and yet grasp the fullness of his love and mercy as evidenced in Christ, we not only are freed from the guilt and shame of our own sins, but we find it possible to forgive others.

I don't want to minimize how hard it can be to truly forgive someone who has done wrong to us. It *is* hard. But God's love for us and his grace extended toward us make forgiveness of even the most heinous offenses possible.

When we freely and fully forgive those who have contributed to our lack of worth, we will experience a true breakthrough in perceiving our worth in God's eyes. When we don't forgive, we're weighed down with a load God never means for us to carry.

When Christian told me he didn't want to forgive his classmate, I decided it was time for us to take a little walk. I went to the pantry and handed Christian a five-pound sack of flour and asked him to carry it for a while.

We hadn't gone far when Christian wanted me to carry the sack for him. "No, it's yours to carry," I explained.

When we had gone a little farther, he asked again. "Mommy, please! The bag is heavy!"

Again, I said "Not yet, Christian."

When we finally reached a certain distance, I told Christian to set the sack of flour down. He did so with a sigh of relief.

You know where I'm going with this, don't you? I explained to Christian that holding on to unforgiveness was just like carrying that bag of flour around all day. Would he really want to carry that weight around all day, every day?

He admitted he wouldn't. Neither do any of us want to carry within us the weight of unforgiveness. It's not our burden to bear. When offense or adversity cause us to hold a grudge in our heart, it's time to lay that load at the feet of Jesus. He can bear the weight; we can't.

One of the greatest lessons I've learned in my life is that God is big enough to handle all the stuff we carry with us. Anger, despair, shame, insecurity, heartbreak, rejection...we can take it all to him. Why? Because he cares for us!

> Cast all your anxiety upon him because he cares for you (1 Peter 5:7).

The Scriptures *promise* that he cares. The Scriptures *promise* that he will uphold us.

Releasing the Hold of Unforgiveness

So how do we fully and finally forgive others?

First, don't look any further than the present moment. Start where you are and how you feel now. And start by telling it all to God. *All of it.* He knows your hurts. Pray it out loud. There is nothing you can say that will shock God. He was there when the offense occurred. Without shifting blame and shame on the other person, simply acknowledge your unforgiveness to God and accept his forgiveness for your part in withholding pardon from your offender.

One of my "Job's comforters" during the dark days of my depression didn't understand my pain. When I longed for help and comfort, she offered accusations. There must be sin in my life. I wasn't reading the Bible enough. Obviously I had a poor prayer life. On and on it went. She even offered me sympathy over my supposed loss of faith.

Wow. Had I really lost my faith? If only she knew that in a very real way God was deepening my faith by allowing me to go through this bleak and lonely night!

Like me, when you go through deep, deep waters, you will have your Job's comforters too. One way I've come to forgive them is to consider that I don't know what's going on in their own lives. I don't know what past, present, or future pathways are part of their journey. Perhaps when I was very young, I might have felt the same way about a woman so desperately depressed she needed to be hospitalized and given a prescription to regain her balance.

I knew I had to forgive this woman, so I tried. But as I began to pray, I felt nothing. *Nothing.* Then slowly—and I do mean *slooooowly*—my prayers changed. After weeks and then months, I finally reached a place where my prayers were tear-stained sobs of intercession for my friend to be blessed.

If I had waited to *feel* forgiveness, nothing would have changed. I might be still carrying that sack of flour today (and it wasn't the five-pounder Christian carried!).

How long have you been lugging around a sack of flour called unforgiveness?

If it's been a long burden-bearing journey, don't feel bad. I'm a slow learner too. I wish I could say my forgiveness of my Job's comforter was a lesson permanently learned. It wasn't.

The Fullness of Forgiveness

I'll never forget my first solo tour of America as a young contemporary Christian artist. I had my British band with me and the tour was a great success. It was hard for some of these guys who were married and had families at home to be away from them for almost six weeks, so I was very excited to pay them and send them home with bonus checks.

That's when everything fell apart. I discovered on the last day of the tour that the tour promoter had left with all the money and had paid no one. When I finally reached him by phone he told me that there was nothing I could do. If I tried to sue him he would file for bankruptcy and start up again under a new name. I was stunned. He was supposed to be a Christian! I flew home to London and sold my house so that I could pay all of those who had worked so hard and for so long with me.

I was angry and hurt. Every time I tried to pray I could feel the waters of bitterness rise inside me, and I knew I didn't want to live like that. So I made a decision. Rather than dwell on the fact that this man took all our money, I determined instead to release it to the Lord and let go of it. I thought this was the end of it, but I had a lot to learn about true forgiveness.

A few years later I was in Estes Park, Colorado, for the annual Christian Artist Retreat. I was hurrying to a class I was teaching when I looked up and saw my former tour manager walking toward me. He saw me at the same moment I saw him and he turned and ran. I was shocked by the anger I felt rising to the surface again after all these years. I dropped to my knees on the ground and asked the Lord why I was still carrying this when I believed I had given it to him.

Immediately the Holy Spirit spoke deep in my heart. "You brought me the offense but you never brought me the offender."

Of course! It can be easy to keep hold of our burden, even when we are weary. But God asks us to release our tight grip on our pain and on those who caused it. I realized that I had not experienced the fullness of forgiveness because I had not fully forgiven!

> God asks us to release our tight grip on our pain and on those who caused it.

There and then I lifted this man up to the throne of grace and asked God to move in his life. I felt something under my left knee cutting into my skin. It was a small pebble. I picked it up and put it in my pocket. I carry it to this day everywhere I go. It is a small, round reminder of a large spiritual principle, "Let any one of you who is without sin be the first to throw a stone!" (John 8:7).

Since God chose you to be the holy people he loves, you must clothe yourselves with tenderhearted mercy, kindness, humility, gentleness, and patience. Make allowance for each other's faults, and forgive anyone who offends you. Remember, the Lord forgave you, so you must forgive others (Colossians 3:12-13 NLT).

Lay It Down in Love

My friend Thelma Wells has every right to be bitter. She was born out of wedlock to a young, crippled black girl. Thelma's grandmother was ashamed of her and locked her in a closet for hours on end. As with many African-Americans of her generation, Thelma was the victim of racial discrimination, including being tossed out of a secretarial college because she wasn't white.

But Thelma had the blessing of a great-grandmother who loved her. Because she was able to be loved, she was able to forgive. Today Thelma is one of the most passionate people-lovers I know. She has not allowed the poison of unforgiveness to imprison her.

If forgiving others is hard, sometimes forgiving ourselves is even harder. But until we can forgive ourselves, I doubt we can truly forgive others.

I believe the problem of unforgiveness is an epidemic in the Body of Christ and has, in many ways, crippled it. Just as forgiveness frees us individually, so too can the Body of Christ be free by learning to forgive.

We also become a better model of God's love to the world when we exhibit forgiveness.

The weight of unforgiveness of others or ourselves is too much for us to bear. We weren't built for that kind of burden. Lay yours down. I ask you in Jesus's name to lay it down now.

Prayer Invitation

Perhaps you've presented the offenses of those who have wronged you to the Lord...but have you brought the offenders to him? Name those who have offended you and pray for them. Not just a superficial "God bless 'em!" but pray for God to draw close to them. Keep praying for these people until you sense in your spirit a freedom from the pain of their offense.

Also, is there someone you need to write a letter to? You may not mail it—in fact, the person you're writing to may be long gone—but it's still important for you to put the freeing words of forgiveness on paper.

6

When the Past Nips at Our Heels

When you follow Christ, it must be a total burning of all your bridges behind you.

BILLY GRAHAM

I'm not particularly good at bridge burning. That should be apparent by the way the events of my childhood followed me into my adult years. Do you, like me, sometimes keep one eye on the rearview mirror of the past?

We're not alone in this. At our conferences I often meet women who still carry the baggage of unresolved pasts, some of which are truly awful. Events that still pain them years, even decades later. Some tell me about the abuse they suffered as a child. Others freely admit mistakes they made that caused them endless agony. The adultery. The divorce. The abortion. The betrayal of a friend. The relationship that ended badly. The auto accident she caused.

Our ability to forgive others can be closely connected to whether or not we have dealt with our own haunted past. Sadly, one of the consequences of a hurtful past is that we stay stuck in our pain and don't move ahead. We don't heal. Sometimes the wound may start to heal, but then something comes along to remind us of our pain. It's as though we've pulled the scab off the wound and the healing must begin again. (Another tactic of the enemy: keeping old wounds festering.)

The Birth of Unworthiness

Even when a past trauma or loss wasn't our fault, the long-term effects can debilitate us for years. For me, the sudden death of my father through suicide was a big game-changer. And part of the tragedy was that Dad knew and understood what was happening to him. It wasn't his fault...and it wasn't mine. And yet it happened and it affected me for a long time. Before his death, I had been a carefree daredevil of a girl. After his death, I became more withdrawn, reserved, fearful.

This was also when I became very concerned about pleasing God. In my youthful naïveté, I simply decided to become the perfect Christian girl. If I succeeded, God would continue to love me. If I failed, God, like my father, would be angry with me. I couldn't bear that. Not after losing my father's love. So I tried very hard to please God in every way I could think of. Not just God, but people too. People-pleasing became my way of life. If others approved of me, I could approve of myself. If others were disappointed in me, I was disappointed. And, by extension, God was also disappointed in me. It was a pattern I carried through my teen years into adulthood. When we are so busy trying to make our own paths to acceptance, we don't notice that God is eagerly calling us to him.

> When we are so busy trying to make our own paths to acceptance, we don't notice that God is eagerly calling us to him.

Because I kept looking for a sense of value in the wrong places, sometimes even doing the right thing furthered my feelings of worthlessness. On my first date with a very popular boy, I was thrilled he had chosen *me*. The thrill left me quickly as he attempted to unbutton my blouse. My incensed response led him to spread the rumor around school that I was a frigid little nun. That was humiliating! How that undermined my sense of worth. Not just in my eyes, but in the eyes of others who jumped on the "Sheila Walsh is different, not like us" bandwagon.

Maybe you can relate to that. Childhood taunts can stay with you through the years. Perhaps you were always the last one chosen for the team. The wallflower at the dance. The girl from the poor side of town—or on the contrary—the favored one from the upper crust in town. Either way, the names can stay with us and contribute to the people we become as adults.

Faced with Pain, Graced with Mercy

God has his merciful ways of forcing us to face the trauma of the past. For me it was that painful diagnosis of clinical depression.

I say this event was "merciful" on God's part because it caused me to at last drop the performance mask. God seems to work rather well with us when we're in ruins. When I could no longer find acceptance with God or with people through performance, I was set free to simply be loved by God, even (or perhaps especially) in my desperate condition.

When some women look at their past—particularly those who came of age during the sexual revolution—they experience afresh the guilt, shame, and regret for sexual sins in which they participated. The guilt and shame are reminders of our unworthiness to be fully loved by God. In fact, for many young women their dabbling in sexual sin was an attempt to be found worthy by someone whose opinion they thought really mattered.

Far too many young women have become sexually promiscuous in their search for worth. A young woman—or a woman of any age for that matter—who is fully grounded in God's love for her will not seek acceptance through the sexual advances of a man. And that's such an exercise in futility anyway. No man—no other person—can ever give us the sense of worthiness that God's love offers.

Think for a moment about some of the women of the Bible who had a less-than-perfect sexual past. Consider Rahab the harlot. Or the woman Jesus encountered at the well. Or the woman taken in adultery who was about to be stoned. Or the woman who broke the alabaster jar of oil to anoint Jesus. Which of these women was not forgiven of her past?

All of them were!

Isn't it strange how we can read about those women and appreciate their forgiveness for past sins and then look at our own past sins with unbelief? We have such a hard time imagining grace for our own sins or failures, don't we?

Reminders of Past Hurts

Letting go of a painful past isn't easy. Especially when the pain wasn't your fault. And especially when your pain will, by necessity, continue to affect your present and your future.

I'd like to tell you about a woman I met after one of our conferences. She had a past that severely affected her present and future. I noticed her in line at a book signing after the evening meeting. It was her face that caught my attention. Shocked me, actually.

She had clearly been a beautiful woman at one point, but half of her face was missing. When I asked if she could share what happened, she told me she had been shot by a stranger who had broken in to her house. She had undergone 32 surgeries and said, "I used to look a lot worse, if you can believe it!"

A long and grace-filled chat followed. I had to know more about her—and especially how she had coped with a tragedy that would send most of us down a deep tunnel of despair.

"It was Christ's love," she said. "When you've spent your life determining your worth by your appearance, and then you lose that, you have to find a new way of measuring your worth. I came to realize that Christ loved the real me, not the outer appearance of me. He loved me before the shooting and he loves me no less now." Through a horrific tragedy, this woman discovered the secret of self-worth: Any measurement of our value apart from Christ's love for us *as we are* is a false measurement and must be rejected. God loves you just as you are, right here and now. Anything else we tell ourselves is a lie.

> God loves you just as you are, right here and now. Anything else we tell ourselves is a lie.

This woman's past would always be a part of her present and future. Thankfully, she learned how to allow that horrific past to pave a new way of measuring her worth. A way that was contrary to the world's standards of value. The world assigns worth to outward beauty, but God doesn't.

God Sees the Heart

When Samuel the prophet was looking over Jesse's sons to anoint a future king of Israel, God told him, "Do not look at his appearance or at his physical stature...For the LORD does not see as man sees; for man looks at the outward appearance, but the LORD looks at the heart" (1 Samuel 16:7 NKJV).

Then, in the New Testament, the apostle Peter reminds women, "Don't be concerned about the outward beauty of fancy hairstyles, expensive jewelry, or beautiful clothes. You should clothe yourselves instead with the beauty that comes from within, the unfading beauty of a gentle and quiet spirit, which is so precious to God" (1 Peter 3:3-4 NLT).

Our worth is from God and God alone. Why then do we so often trust our sense of worth to a world that bombards us with unattainable images of so-called perfect women? The truth is that perfection is a myth, pure and simple, but godly beauty is a truth that never fades. When I read that it's precious to God, I want that. I want to cultivate a life that brings him honor and pleasure, don't you?

Oh, if only we could learn to resist our culture's measurements of worth! If we could refuse to accept our dress size as a symbol of our worth. Or our hair color. Or our wrinkles. Or our bank account. Or our professional status. Or our family background.

None of these matter to God.

If we could just stop looking at ourselves in the distorted funhouse mirror of the world's values and see us as God sees us—as a treasure of his creation.

This inspiring woman at the book signing had more to teach me about a subject we discussed in chapter five. She told me, "The other important factor was for me to forgive. Not just the man who shot me, but also myself. I saw that I could have beaten myself up for the rest of my life for living with a false measurement of physical beauty for so long." What an awakening! To discover through such a tragedy that her measuring rod of worth had been false for so long.

She taught me something else too. God could have changed this young woman's circumstances. He could have prevented her attack. He could have had surgeons successfully rebuild her face. But he didn't do that. What happened instead was that he changed *her*. That's a lesson for us: If we cannot change our adverse circumstances, we must pray that God will change us.

> If we cannot change our
> adverse circumstances,
> we must pray that
> God will change us.

You're a Prize—Past and All

In addition to physical beauty, our culture assigns more worth to youth than to the aged. Sadly, I know many older Christian women who try to resist aging in a way that can be very unhealthy. We all want to look our best, but if our aim is to hang on to our fleeting youth and thus be considered worthy in the eyes of the world, we're bypassing God's measurement of worth. The truth is, we're not letting go of the past either, though in a very different way.

What of your past? Can you think of things that have profoundly affected the way you see yourself? Although it would be wrong to dismiss those very important events in your life, neither is it wise to allow them to continue to fill our minds and feed our doubts. To live fully and worthy will necessarily mean we're willing to move on from the past, no matter what.

Our past—whether good or bad—is just a road behind us that has led us to today. The roads may look different, but they are all designed to lead us to the *exact same truth* about ourselves. Whether it's clinical depression, the loss of physical beauty, or overt rejection by someone whose acceptance is important to us, each of these divergent paths all come together at the foot of the cross. It's there and only there that we find our true worth. Oh, that we could discover this without such painful journeys! God in his wisdom must know what it takes for each of us to arrive at the foot of the cross. We must, therefore, never resent the means by which God shows us how dearly he values us. We are his prize possession! Each of us!

Prayer Invitation

This might seem a strange thing to admit, but some of my best conversations have been with myself. Yes, I talk to myself. Often. I highly recommend it. In fact, let's do a little self-talking now about our past. You know mine. I don't know yours. Tell me about it. Out loud. (Hopefully you're alone right now!) Just name your regrets, one by one. Both those that you're accountable for and those that you never chose to experience, but which are nonetheless part of your past, and possibly your present and future.

As you name these regrets, let your words carry each one of them to the cross. Let that be their final resting place. The next time one of those painful memories rears its ugly head, remind yourself that that awful event from your past has been lifted from your shoulders. You bear it no more.

Then instead of listening to the replay of that old tape in your head, turn on a new tape. Talk to yourself about the forgiveness you have in Christ. Remind yourself that God wastes nothing. Every event in your past is redeemable.

Take joy in formulating these new tapes. You will want to replay them often!

7

Unmet Expectations

How else but through a broken heart may Lord Christ enter in?

OSCAR WILDE

Is your life turning out the way you expected? If not, is it better or worse than you hoped for?

Many women can trace their frustration with self-worth to unmet expectations. They've become disappointed, either mildly or greatly, with the way events have played out in their life.

Is that you? Are you where you hoped you'd be by this time in your life?

If not, I'd like you to take a lesson from your GPS. If you're like me, when you've set your destination on your GPS and you start out on your trip, it won't be long until a familiar female voice tells you she's "recalculating." Why is this woman you've never met telling you such a thing? It's because you've taken a wrong turn. And to get to your desired destination, she must now redirect you to get back on the right path.

In the same way, God knows our final destination and no matter how many "wrong turns" we make, God can "recalculate" our journey so that we are soon right back where we should be. Your disappointments fall by the wayside as you, by faith, accept God's destination.

With our human perspective, it's difficult for us to understand how God can incorporate our mistakes and utter failures into the very fabric of his plan. But if you belong to him, he is working out the details of your life so that you will arrive at the desired destination. Not necessarily a destination that matched your expectations. An even better one, of course!

The Great Exchange

Often we are hesitant to exchange our expectations for what God is leading us through. Perhaps we dreamed of the perfect marriage or the brilliant career or obedient kids who would grow to be strong, useful Christians, but our realities are different. Maybe our marriage isn't perfect. Our career may have been sidelined for reasons beyond our control. Our children may be rebelling, causing us great emotional pain. Perhaps a breast cancer diagnosis came out of nowhere and we are reeling from the news.

Many events, people, and circumstances can enter our path and change our course. But one important step in our transition from our wild-eyed youth to a mature, productive adulthood is coming to grips with the fact that our Plan A might not even be God's Plan Z.

It has been hard for me to accept many of the unexpected turns in the road of my life. My father's death was only the beginning. As a successful, ministry-minded young woman, I certainly wouldn't have foreseen clinical depression as something God would use to further my ministry. (Who would include *that* in their Plan A?) My later-in-life entry into marriage and motherhood, the self-doubts, the many ups and downs of life have all been a part of God's plan.

I've had more than my share of surprises—many of which have been wonderful. For instance, *my* Plan A didn't include the privilege of ministering to more than five million women over the past three decades. It didn't include meeting many of these women one-on-one, allowing me to touch the tender sore spots in their life. But God, in recalculating my journey, had a better plan for me all along.

Truth be told, as a teenager, I wanted to be a nurse. And then I happened to visit our pastor's wife in the hospital as her bandages were being changed. That ended my nursing dreams.

A missionary to India! Yes, that's what I'd be. So off to seminary I went. Up went the map of India on my dorm wall. And up went my tear-filled prayers for India. Oh yes, surely God was leading me to India.

Would you believe that all these years later, India is one of the few countries I've never visited? God had a different plan. My expectation was dashed. But it was only dashed because it wasn't the destiny God knew would fulfill me. Oh, be thankful your expectations were unmet! Where might you be now if God gave you what you thought you wanted?

Give Your "If Only" to God

Unmet expectations can shake us to the core. It's easier when we're young and just beginning, but as the years go by and we look back, we may mistakenly grieve what might have been...*if only*.

- If only I hadn't married.
- If only I had married.
- If only I was smarter.
- If only I was beautiful.
- If only I got that job.
- If only I hadn't been abused.
- If only I didn't wrestle with depression.

With God, there are no *if only*s. Isaac's son Joseph would never have chosen his horrible years of imprisonment in a foreign land. But we never hear of Joseph saying "If only I hadn't been so prideful with my brothers." Ruth's loss of her husband wasn't her Plan A. But in her desire to return with her mother-in-law, Naomi, to Judah, she embarked on a new life that put her in the ancestry of Jesus. The Bible is full of stories of men and women with unmet expectations. Ask Sarah. Talk to Job. Or Hannah. How about Jonah? Peter?

In looking back, I'm sure each of them would tell us that the road to God's will might very well be in the opposite direction of our expectations.

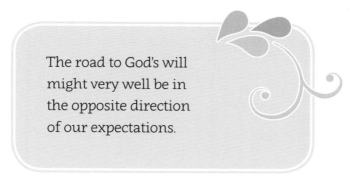

The road to God's will might very well be in the opposite direction of our expectations.

Many times expectations are born as a result of taking our cues from either the culture's expectations or from our comparisons with others. Going down either road will have God's "recalculating" voice coming across our inner GPS at the earliest possible moment.

Frankly, I have a hunch about comparisons. I suspect that many of the women we compare ourselves to are comparing themselves to others they envy. Maybe even you!

Like you, they probably have an internal list of what they wished they looked like or the talents they'd give anything to have. Sometimes I think every woman carries this secret list of comparisons or her weaknesses in her mind. Isn't it interesting and telling that not many women I know carry around an internal list of their strengths or the reasons they're valued by God?

Wouldn't you love to live in a world where women (and men!) aren't caught up in the comparison game? You can live in such a world, you know. You can simply stop playing the game yourself.

The Offering of Your Yes

I've learned that happiness comes from saying yes to God. And saying yes to God sometimes means saying yes to many things we want to say no to. Saying yes (through tears) to the child you've lost. Saying yes to the husband you have, not the husband you thought you had. Yes to the lost job (with the hope of something better), yes to the difficult person God has sent into your life. Yes to the aging parent who needs your care.

No, life isn't fair as we count fairness. But there's a deeper truth that trumps the "fairness" of life issue. That truth is that God is just, good, sovereign, and he makes no mistakes. I don't know what God is calling you to embrace, but I do know the God who is doing the calling. We can trust him with our next steps.

> I don't know what God is calling you to embrace, but I do know the God who is doing the calling.

One woman I met at a Women of Faith conference came to Christ because she finally said yes to the worst thing imaginable for a mother. Her young son contracted a fatal blood disease. She was an agnostic at best, "never giving God much thought," she said. As she watched her three-year-old son grow weaker and weaker, she turned to her only hope: the God she hadn't believed in.

She told me, "I began to pray then—and read the Bible. My prayers were for God to simply help us." Then, through her tears she said, "When I finally handed my son to Christ, I handed him all of me too."

This woman made an offering to God that day of her faith, her heart, her life.

She said yes.

Will you say yes too?

Prayer Invitation

I asked you at the beginning of this chapter about your unmet expectations. Now I'm asking you to notice God's hope in those disappointments. And I want you to make a decision to see him in your future unmet expectations. When those occur, I want you to hear God's voice in your inner GPS say, "Recalculating."

Consider making Psalm 62:5 your life verse as it pertains to expectations: "My soul, wait silently for God alone, for my expectation is from him" (NKJV).

Pray now to release hold of your expectations (past and current ones) so you can receive God's expectations and plans for your life.

8

Stormy Weather Ahead

Fiery trials make golden Christians.
CHARLES SPURGEON

Along our journey together, you've thought seriously about your secret self, your fear of rejection, God's love, forgiveness, and overcoming your past. I hope you've also let go of many of the things we've discussed and are focused on a future of worthiness in Christ. Now we can explore what it means to move forward in your worth and with a deeper understanding of God's plan for your life.

Now, I may have to call this a spoiler alert, but once you've come to accept (and revel in) your worth in God's eyes, you will still face new storms in the months and years ahead. Being grounded in God's love for us is not a deterrent to the trials. It is, however, a safeguard as a storm passes through.

And storms *do* pass through. They blow in with dark clouds, pouring rain, lightning, and thunder that scares some of us out of our wits—and then moves on. I've never known of a storm that didn't eventually move on. Life is like that. The storms you are going through right now *will* pass.

The problem is that too often storms serve as a setback to our faith. Doubts arise with the dark clouds—doubts that try to tell us, *I haven't changed at all. I'm the same unlovely, unlovable person I've always been.*

More lies. The enemy knows that during the storms of life we're more susceptible to his deceits. So when storms come, we need to be prepared. Just as we would if the Channel 5 meteorologist warned us of an approaching tornado.

Your Personal Storms

I don't know what your personal, future storms will look like. You probably don't either. More rejection? Another broken relationship? Perhaps a child who wanders from the faith? A mate who wants out of the marriage? The loss of a job or a home? Troublesome lab tests?

That last one was one of my recent storms. I really didn't see it coming.

I woke up in the middle of the night in more pain than I have ever experienced apart from childbirth. I was doubled over as the pain shot through me in waves. Finally, I had to awaken Barry and ask him to drive me to the emergency room. Once there, the nurse put in an IV and began to give me some pain medication, but it barely took the edge off. After several scans, I was finally diagnosed with a kidney stone. I had no idea that something so small could cause so much pain. A urologist said he thought the stone would pass on its own and was about to send me home when he looked again at something on the x-ray. He added, "I don't like the look of that. You should have your doctor check it out."

I'm not proud to share this, but the truth is, I forgot all about whatever it was he saw. I'm usually more vigilant but, as you know, life gets busy and making dinner, doing laundry, traveling, speaking, yada yada yada...well, a few months passed. When it was time for my annual physical, I did remember to take the charts the urologist had given me. When my doctor understood how much time had passed, she wasn't happy at all. She explained that I had a growth the size of a plum on my left ovary. If I were twenty years old, then it wouldn't be much of a concern; but because I was in menopause, it wasn't good. She told me that she wanted me in surgery the following week.

I was a little shaken by her intensity but I asked if it would be possible to wait just one more week. I was about to tape an eight-week Bible Study in Austin, Texas and the film crew was already on the way. She approved one week, but not a day more. Each day as I filmed the sessions the thought of the upcoming surgery sat like a troublesome bird on my shoulder.

Peace in the Chaos

When we had one morning left to film and I got up early to watch the sunrise over the lake, I noticed I had a message from my doctor that hadn't been there the night before. She asked me to call her no matter the time. She told me that she had shown my film to a colleague and was moving my surgery to a different hospital. I knew then she believed the tumor was cancerous. I thanked her and told her I'd be there bright and early on the Monday morning.

One session left to film, just one. And now these dark clouds of uncertainty were gathering more quickly. And yet...I had peace. Despair turned to faith. As the sun began to rise above the lake I got down on my knees and prayed a prayer I've never prayed before.

"Father, all of this is a surprise to me but not to you. I know you're in control no matter how things feel. So here's my heart, Lord. I want whatever will bring you the most glory. If it will bring you more glory for this to be cancer, because I might find myself in a room with a woman who doesn't know you, then I say yes! If it will bring you more glory for this to be benign, then I say yes to that too. You have been so faithful to me through all those years. I trust you with what I can see and what is hidden from me. I love you! Amen."

Monday morning I was wheeled into the operating room. The last thing I remember is a young surgical nurse taking my hand and saying just one word: "Jesus."

When I woke up in the recovery room the smile on my doctor's face spoke volumes. "It was bigger than I thought—the size of a grapefruit—but it was benign."

I was grateful, deeply grateful, but here's what I know is true: No matter the outcome, God's grace and mercy, his relentless love and companionship, can and will hold me. It will hold you too.

One important part of preparing for a storm is to believe God has something he wants to accomplish during the storm. Then watch for his hand in it.

Wait and watch. Don't waste the storm. Let it do its work.

> Believe God has something he wants to accomplish during the storm. Then watch for it.

Gather the Spiritual Blessings

How, exactly, do we spiritually make the most of a trial in our life? First, we need to look at any storm as a messenger from God. Often the message is simply, "Trust me in this. You will come through." In that sense, storms can bring blessings to our lives as they build our faith.

As I look back on my diagnosis of clinical depression, I'm reminded of how God has used some of the worst days of my life to bring about blessing. He has used my depression in a way I could never have imagined during the darkest days. To be honest, without my ongoing struggle with depression, I would have nothing to say to you. It was through the darkness that God brought light into my life. Pain is often a means to healing. The surgeon's knife is sharp as it cuts, but without the pain of surgery, there is no healing. So it is with us.

We don't like adversity when it happens, but our response is what determines how the adversity will affect us. At such times, we're tempted to say, "It's not fair!" But what is every mother's response when her child makes the same claim? We often reply, "Life's *not* fair."

No, life isn't fair as we count fairness. But there's a deeper truth that trumps the "fairness" of life issue. That truth is that God is just, good, sovereign, and he makes no mistakes. Even more, he makes pain work for our good when we look through the eyes of faith.

The second way to understand the blessings of your difficulty or changed expectation is to allow God's Word to be made real.

In the Bible we read about real people with real problems like our own. They faced hurricane-force storms just as we do. Job? Sarah? Ruth? David? Peter? And how about Jesus? Temptations, slow-learning disciples, angry Pharisees, and finally death on the cross. Later, the apostle Paul would recount his storms—some of which were literal as he faced shipwreck, imprisonment, and great deprivation. During one of his toughest storms, Paul wrote this:

> We are pressed on every side by troubles, but we are not crushed. We are perplexed, but not driven to despair. We are hunted down, but never abandoned by God. We get knocked down, but we are not destroyed. Through

suffering, our bodies continue to share in the death of Jesus so that the life of Jesus may also be seen in our bodies (2 Corinthians 4:8-10 NLT).

It was Paul who faced a trial in the form of "buffeting from Satan," and yet God's message to him during that storm was "My grace is sufficient for you, for my power is made perfect in weakness" (2 Corinthians 12:9).

Your Anchor of Truth

Learn to see every storm as having a positive purpose. Satan's purpose is to cause us to fear and doubt. God's purpose is for us to rely on his strength and come out the other side with more resilient faith.

With every storm, remember this. No matter how things seem, no matter how we feel, these things remain true:

In the darkest night, we are never alone.

God's love is always surrounding us.

He is in control.

He is faithful.

He will never leave us or forsake us.

Reflect on these next two verses as you consider your trial and the blessings that are arising even as the wind blows.

> Cast all your anxiety on him because he cares for you (1 Peter 5:7).

Do not fear, for I am with you; do not be dismayed, for I am your God. I will strengthen you and help you; I will uphold you with my righteous right hand (Isaiah 41:10).

A woman of faith is one who, when visited by the storms of life, holds fast to the anchor of truth. Although she does not understand everything, her faith is in the finished work of Christ.

Wherever you are today, whatever it is that you've faced or will face, I urge you, friend, to hold fast to the promises of God. You are not alone, even in the darkest of storms. Our God is faithful!

Prayer Invitation

Lord, I don't like storms. I like sunshine and calm. But I know storms are necessary sometimes. Help me be prepared when a fresh storm blows my way. Give me eyes to see your purpose. Allow me to learn the lesson you have for me. Amen.

9

An Eternal Perspective

Begin in mercy a new work of love within me. Say to my soul, "Rise up, my love, my fair one, and come away." Then give me grace to rise and follow Thee up from this.

A.W. TOZER

Can I let you in on a secret? Okay, so it's no secret at all. But it's true and if you've forgotten about it, this is the perfect time to remind you...

Jesus has gone ahead to prepare a place for you. For *you.* He would not do such a thing for someone who has no worth.

Why is that important to remember? Because we are so very short-sighted as we concentrate on the things of this world. Meanwhile, eternity gets lost in the tedium of our to-do lists. We're as slow to remember our purpose here on earth as we are to realize our true worth to God.

For years I struggled with the question of why I was alive. What was my purpose? What should I be *doing* for God's kingdom? But I've come to see that who am I in Christ is all the purpose I need. Once I rest in that, everything else will fall into place as it should. I'm here to receive the love of God and to be an expression of his love to others. With that as my purpose, it really doesn't matter if I sing or teach or counsel women. If I lose my voice, what have I lost really? If my identity is in Christ, my voice is only useful as a temporary tool for ministry. My voice is not who I am. Neither are you the sum of your gifts or accomplishments. And the best way to understand this is to believe that God's love for each of us will never change even if he chooses to redirect us away from our present life. We always have eternity...and eternity is enough.

When the Winds Change

Could you handle a radical change of direction from God? If I knew I could never sing or speak again, I would feel such a profound sense of loss...that is, until I accepted the fact that God doesn't love or need my voice. He loves and needs *me*. With or without my voice.

Remember, I thought I lost everything once already. And to my surprise, that "loss" was actually a true finding. Our present losses are all temporal. Our value is eternal. When we keep our eyes on eternity, we're no longer in such a rush to succeed in this life. We can patiently wait for God's timing in all things.

Our present losses
are all temporal. Our
value is eternal.

When you plant zucchini seeds in your garden, do you expect to wake up the next morning and find plump, full-grown squashes ready for the picking? No, of course not. We all know that growing vegetables takes time. So does growth in our spiritual life. And so does developing an understanding of our worthiness before God.

We may have a breakthrough moment when we begin to perceive God's deep love for us. But that's just a beginning. From there, we must continue to grow in his love. We accept the water of his Word, we daily yield ourselves to the Holy Spirit, we become transformed by his presence in us. And we understand that our circumstances change, but God doesn't.

Your Value as a Masterpiece

God's ways with us are not quick ways (oh, how we wish they were!). God is often slow, patient, just as an artist is slow and painstaking over the future masterpiece on his easel. Though God is slow in his work, he is always present as he works. We are never left alone as his paintbrush moves deftly over the canvas.

Understanding this truth changed my life. For so many years I had been doing things for God and failing miserably. But when I realized that we can't do things for God, we can only do things *in* him, that's when I really grew in my relationship with the Lord.

> We can't do things
> for God; we can only
> do things *in* him.

Shortly after my release from the hospital, a friend of mine commented that I seemed so different from before. "So free," she said. And it was true...I *was* free. God had given me a new life through the odd process of clinical depression. But I understood my friend's reaction when she said, "If that's the only way to get a new life, I think I'll pass."

I totally got it. Who would choose depression as an avenue to a new life? That's the thing about the way God works. It's different for each of us.

Consider this for a moment: Could God be using your struggle to find self-worth as a means of revealing himself to you in a deeper way than if you were brimming with self-assurance and self-acceptance?

Have you thanked God for bringing you to the low valleys so that he might lead you through them and up to the majestic mountain views?

Redeemed and Loved

God wastes nothing. All that happens in our lives can be redeemed. And it's God's will to do the redeeming. Can we honestly read the Bible and not see God's delight in bringing good out of horrible situations? When we read the book of Job, we suffer along with him. What a terrible turn of events for that dear man! But how does the book end?

"Now the Lord blessed the latter days of Job more than his beginning" (Job 42:12 NKJV).

Whatever you've been through, whatever has been at the root of your sense of lack of worth, join me in taking a note from Job. Let's believe our latter days—those from here on out—will be better than our beginning. Our best years are ahead! We will know our worth as daughters of God and we will rejoice in it. We will take joy in knowing we were created to love God and give him pleasure. For fellowship. We were created by God because he wanted each of us to be included in his family. Yes, you and all the other women down through history who have become partakers of His love.

If you had asked me 15 years ago what I wanted, I would've said (and I did on several occasions) that I was hungry to be a woman with a heart on fire for God. My hope wasn't to just gain knowledge about him, but to truly know him and trust him with everything. I didn't want to talk about the love of God; I wanted my life and my heart to be consumed by that love.

That desire is as true now as it was then.

I'm learning to find my worth in God's amazing love for me.

I'm learning to rest in the truth of who his Word says I am.

I'm learning to talk through every little moment of my day with him before I take it out on someone else.

I'm learning to be honest with myself and with others.

I'm learning to be still and know that he is God.

I'm learning to worship in the darkness, trusting God that dawn will come.

I've come to realize that my crazy, unpredictable, yet wonderful life matters to God. He takes me as I am, and in some gloriously redemptive way he finds a will for my life that is perfect to him, though often perplexing to me. And I can live with that.

I believe you can too.

We've had quite a journey together in a short time! As we revisited past hurts, identified our secret selves, and explored our personal storms, God has been with us. He has in his mercy started a new work within us. And he will be with us as we go on from here knowing, believing, and living as radiant women whose worth is found in the unwavering love of our Lord.

Prayer Invitation

Where do you place your hope? And what are you learning as you take each step closer and closer to knowing the God of beginnings as the one who loves you unconditionally? I encourage you to spend time on your knees today praising our merciful God who redeems, committing your every weakness and strength to his purpose and waiting in joyful anticipation for his faithful leading.

My Prayer for You

Father God,

Thank you for this dear reader. Thank you for the time invested to stay the course and follow my thoughts and this winding path of my journey.

But now Father, I pray for her. I ask that you would do what only you can do.

I ask that you would reach deep down into this fragile human heart and speak your words of love and mercy.

I ask for a fresh revelation of your redemptive grace and purpose.

I ask for an overwhelming awareness of the value that you place on this one treasured life.

I ask for everything you long to pour out because you love us.

In Jesus's precious name, amen.

Bestselling author, speaker, and Bible teacher, Sheila Walsh is dedicated to showing what happens when real life meets the Word of God. She's the author of the #1 bestselling line of Christian books for little girls, *Gigi, God's Little Princess*, creator of *5 Minutes with Jesus* and *The Bible Is My Best Friend*, and an accomplished musician. Sheila, her husband, Barry, and their son live in Dallas, Texas.